MW00658221

MY LI
IKIGAI
JOURNAL

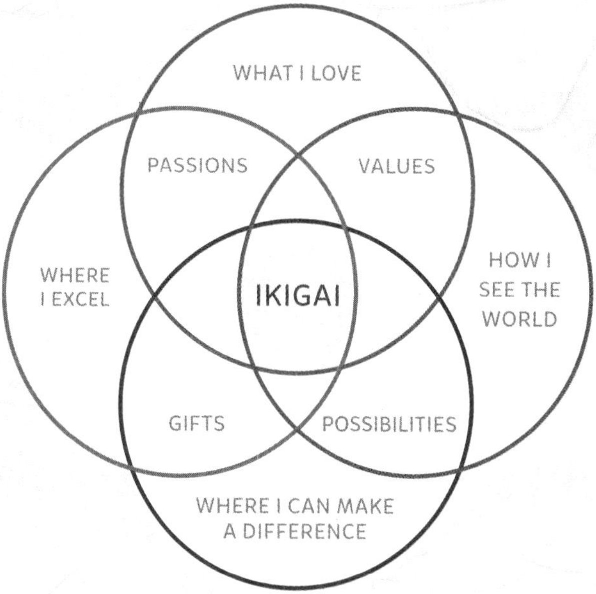

A Journey into the Japanese Secret to Living a Long, Happy, Purpose-Filled Life

· AMANDA KUDO ·

Castle Point Books
New York

MY LITTLE IKIGAI JOURNAL Copyright © 2018 by St. Martin's Press.
All rights reserved. Printed in the United States of America. For information, address St. Martin's Press, 175 Fifth Avenue, New York, N.Y. 10010.

www.stmartins.com
www.castlepointbooks.com

The Castle Point Books trademark is owned by Castle Point Publishing, LLC.
Castle Point books are published and distributed by St. Martin's Press.

ISBN 978-1-250-19981-2 (trade paperback)

Design by Katie Jennings Campbell
Composition by Joanna Williams
Images used under license from Shutterstock.com.

Our books may be purchased in bulk for promotional, educational, or business use. Please contact your local bookseller or the Macmillan Corporate and Premium Sales Department at 1-800-221-7945, extension 5442, or by e-mail at MacmillanSpecialMarkets@macmillan.com.

First Edition: September 2018

10 9 8 7 6 5 4 3 2

CONTENTS

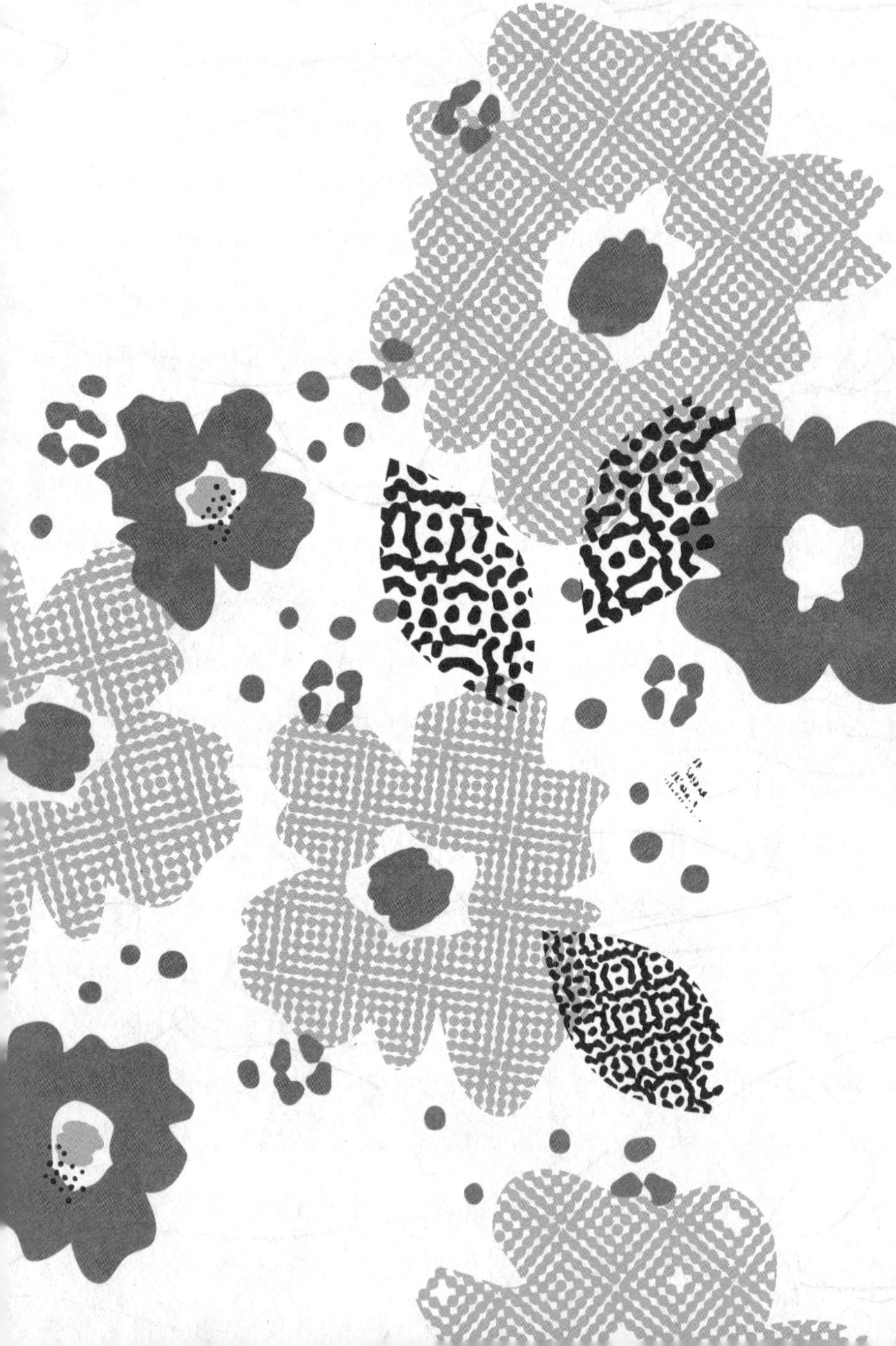

DISCOVERING YOUR IKIGAI

Learn how finding and following your purpose can bring you amazing health and happiness!

The purpose of life is
to discover your gift.
The work of life is
to develop it.
The meaning of life is
to give your gift away.

DAVID VISCOTT

WHAT'S MISSING?

What would it take to wake each morning

with physical and mental energy to surge into the day? Knowing that the time ahead of you is filled with purpose and possibility? The secret that leads to the difference: discovering (or reconnecting with) your ikigai.

You can eat healthy foods, commit to regular physical activity, and care for yourself with stress-relief techniques. But if you aren't connected to your ikigai, you're missing an essential key to health and happiness. The Japanese word *ikigai* translates as "reason for being." You also can think of it as the "reason to get out of bed." Everyone, according to Japanese culture, has an ikigai, and staying true to it in everything we do is the secret to a long, happy life. People of retirement age in Japan don't put their feet up: they continue to pursue their ikigai, which leads to fulfillment and contentment. It's no wonder that a village in Okinawa, one of the Japanese islands, boasts some of the most long-lived people in the world. But it's a universal truth: Living with purpose brings amazing benefits. Experts who study centenarians—people who live to be one hundred years old and beyond—believe that knowing your sense of purpose is worth up to seven additional years of life!

The best part: Discovering your ikigai can be as simple as spending a few minutes each day focusing on *you*. *My Little Ikigai Journal* will be your guide through:

- Your Passions—What You Love
- Your Gifts—Where You Excel
- Your Values—How You See the World
- Your Possibilities—Where You Can Make a Difference

The place where these circles come together is your ikigai. Let it be a gift of health, happiness, and life-changing purpose you give yourself as you journey through these pages!

YOUR PASSIONS

What You Love

Little prompts can help you identify what truly makes you feel alive.

YOUR DAY, YOUR WAY

Imagine you have an entire day to spend any way you'd like. The only guideline: Your choices must bring you pleasure and true fulfillment, not simply help you "catch up" (with sleep or paperwork) or check off items from your to-do list. How does the day play out?

LIVING THE MOMENT

Find a photo in which you're smiling or laughing (not posed!). Secure it below, and recall what you were doing, or with whom, that filled you with such joy and energy.

IMAGINE THE ITINERARY

When you travel to a new place, what are the first things you check out and want to know more about?

- ○ Restaurants and cafés
- ○ Art museums and studios
- ○ Live-music venues
- ○ Parks and natural wonders
- ○ Libraries and universities
- ○ Dance clubs
- ○ Sporting events
- ○ Historical and cultural sites
- ○
- ○
- ○

CONVERSATION HEARTS

You're at a party chatting with someone you just met. What topics could you talk about for hours, and what topics make you feel bored or uncomfortable?

LET'S TALK:

....

....

....

....

TIME TO MOVE ON:

....

....

....

....

....

IT'S NEVER TOO LATE

During childhood, when were you at your happiest? Recall a few specific events, activities, or places that bring to mind a feeling of joy or freedom.

What childhood dreams do you still carry that you were never able to fully explore? If you've kept in touch, reach out to childhood friends and ask them what they remember about you as a child—your loves, hopes, and dreams.

There is no passion to be found playing small—in settling for a life that is less than the one you are capable of living.

NELSON MANDELA

THE ROLLER-COASTER EFFECT

Your passions may not lie on a safe, predictable path. Describe a time you stepped out of your comfort zone but came out of the experience with a feeling of excitement, even exhilaration.

Remember your dreams and fight for them.

PAULO COELHO

REVISIT YOUR RESUME

Although passion and purpose may not be fulfilled solely through employment, jobs can give us a taste of what we thrive on and what dulls our senses. What specific activities have you done in a past or current job that you really enjoy and find engaging?

What specific activities have you done in a past or current job that you dislike and never want to do again?

ALL YOU NEED

Our sources of joy are unique and personal. What are 10 things, people, or activities that you could not bear to live a week without?

1.

2.

3.

4.

5.

6.

7.

8.

9.

10.

If you can't figure
out your purpose,
figure out your passion.
For your passion
will lead you right
into your purpose.

T. D. JAKES

SCAN YOUR SHELVES

Consider the books you've read in the past few years and the titles you have on your "want to read" list. Is there a common theme that connects them? Is there a subject you never tire of absorbing or learning more about?

SURROUND YOURSELF WITH SUPPORT

Living a life filled with passion is a goal that isn't always embraced in our culture. But you can strengthen your awareness of passion and value its place in your life's purpose more fully. The secret is the company you keep. How many of your friends and family are following their passions? How can you spend more time with people who inspire your pursuit of passion and purpose over wealth and material measures of achievement?

CHANNEL YOUR ENVY

Is there a part of someone's life you've always admired? A hobby, volunteer position, job, or skill you'd love to have? Act on your envy—ask your contact when you can spend a day shadowing her or when she can help you dabble in what she knows.

MAKE THE PLAN:

....

....

....

....

CAPTURE THE RESULTS:

....

....

....

....

First, think.
Second, dream.
Third, believe.
And, finally, dare.

WALT DISNEY

A PERFECT MATCH

Our passions may be clearer to others than to us. What present have you received that made you instantly amazed at how well the giver knows you?

ENTER THE FANDOM

What things, activities, or topics do your friends and family tease you for being obsessed with? Be honest!

WHAT TIME IS IT?

Recall the last instance when you completely lost track of time while engaged in an activity. (Sleeping doesn't count!) What were you doing?

When you do things from your soul, you feel a river moving in you, a joy.

JALAL AL-DIN RUMI

COME IN, WE'RE OPEN!

Imagine you are undertaking a new business venture: opening a restaurant of your own. What tasks do you feel confident and excited about handling on your own? What roles will you rely on others for?

	All Me!	Not Me!
Planning the menu	○	○
Preparing the food	○	○
Choosing the aesthetic or decor	○	○
Doing renovations or building projects	○	○
Drumming up PR	○	○
Designing a logo and signage	○	○
Handling the finances	○	○
Greeting the customers	○	○

RIGHT WHERE YOU BELONG

What are some favorite places in your life—spaces where you feel at home away from your actual home?

Are there qualities they share—near or away from people, indoors or out, quiet or bustling?

The little things?
The little moments?
They aren't little.

JON KABAT-ZINN

START LITTLE, THINK BIG

Make a list of 10 "little" things or moments that brought a smile to your face in the past few weeks.

1.

2.

3.

4.

5.

6.

7.

8.

9.

10.

GET A LITTLE CRAZY

Have you ever told someone about a plan you were making or a dream you had, only to hear the response, "You're/That's crazy!"? Don't let labels wipe that idea away; capture the thought here. Did you follow through? If so, how did it turn out? If not, why not—and is it still something you think about?

Sanity and happiness are an impossible combination.

MARK TWAIN

THE CHECKBOOK TRUTH

Although no one loves paying taxes, medical expenses, or debts, other categories that pop up frequently in financial statements may say something about your passions. What rough percentages do these categories make up?

Adventure

Art

Books

Charity

Clothing

Education

Entertainment

Fitness

Food

Furnishings

Music

Pets

Sports

Technology

Travel

Vehicles

GOOD AND TIRED

When was the last time you were totally exhausted physically yet completely at rest in spirit?

I'm tired,
but proud.

NORMAN ROCKWELL

KEY INGREDIENTS

Setting aside time and money, what do you feel you need more of in your life to be truly happy?

YOUR GIFTS

Where You Excel

Simple questions and exercises help you recognize your skills and offerings.

ACCORDING TO PLAN

Each week, you complete a ton of seemingly simply tasks—from paying bills to preparing meals, from checking in on friends and family to cleaning house. What tasks always go smoothly for you, and which are a struggle or burden?

SMOOTH SAILING:

THE STRUGGLE IS REAL:

CAPTURE THE COMPLIMENTS

Think of as many times as you can when someone said, "Wow, you're really good at that!" What were you doing? Capture all those talents—big and small.

THE IMPORTANCE OF CLASS

What skills have you ever taught someone? It could be playing an instrument or sport, speaking a language, using an app, driving a car, cooking a meal, sewing on a button, even learning how to take a deep breath. No matter how complex or simple, jot it down.

YOUR OWN SUPERHERO

Think of a time you felt super-confident, like you could accomplish anything, even if for only a moment. What were you doing?

YOUR TOP FIVE

List the five accomplishments that fill you with the most pride. Keep in mind that sometimes the most fulfilling things bring little recognition and yield no monetary results. So be honest—you're not in a job interview; you're on a quest to discover purpose.

1.

2.

3.

4.

5.

To be yourself
in a world that is
constantly trying to
make you something
else is the greatest
accomplishment.

RALPH WALDO EMERSON

NOT *THAT!*

What's your biggest area of procrastination in a typical week? Think about that chore or task that fills you with dread.

....

....

....

....

....

....

....

....

....

In case you haven't already guessed, this area of procrastination is generally *not* a skill set! It's good to know what roads not to head down as well.

FOLLOW THAT TRAIN

In what areas have you been trained or educated in any way—from one-day workshops to full educational degrees?

ANSWER THE CALL

Your phone rings or a text notification sounds with a request from a friend or family member. What are they likely turning to you for? What do others feel you have to offer?

THE GIFT OTHERS CAN GIVE

Sometimes we don't see in ourselves what others can see in us. Ask someone close to you who sees you in a positive light to recount your gifts. Record the responses here.

A HAT INVENTORY

Consider all the hats you wear in your life. Your roles might look something like: marketing rep, parent, spouse, dog walker, chef, driver, counselor, family photographer. Put a star next to the hats you enjoy wearing the most; mark an X next to the hats you'd love to toss.

Don't second-guess every decision you make—you'll go crazy. If you like the hat, wear it.

UNKNOWN

I am what
is mine.
Personality is
the original
personal property.

NORMAN O. BROWN

JUST THE WAY YOU ARE

Think of the five aspects of your personality for which you are most grateful. Maybe it's your creativity, listening skills, sense of adventure, clearheadedness under pressure, discipline to accomplish hard things. List what's true for you.

EYES ON THE PRIZE

List any awards you have won. Think beyond academic and athletic achievements. Were you named as "most likely to" in your yearbook? There's often truth even in the humor of all-in-fun awards given to you by family, friends, and coworkers.

Certificate of Achievement

GRADE A

Think back to all the different kinds of tests you've taken in your life—from school and special certifications to driving. Are there ones you passed with flying colors?

WHERE HAVE YOU BEEN?

One of the greatest gifts we can share is empathy, understanding the path another has traveled. What challenges or struggles have you conquered in your life—or are you in the process of navigating right now? Which of those experiences may be able to help someone else?

The greatest accomplishment is not in never falling, but in rising again after you fall.

VINCE LOMBARDI

IN YOUR HANDS

What homemade gifts have you given throughout your life? For each one, consider whether you enjoyed the process of creating it and what inspired you to make the gift.

LITTLE VICTORIES

What experiences today made you most relate to the statement, "Well, that went well"? Reflect on what led to that result and feeling.

THE "EASY" BUTTON

Everyone has abilities that seem to come with ease. What kinds of skills or knowledge have always come naturally to you—without much coaching or studying?

There is an amazing power getting to know your inner self and learning how to use it and not fight with the world.

JUHI CHAWLA

One person
with passion
is better than
forty people
merely interested.

E. M. FORSTER

A SENSE OF BELONGING

Pull out those membership cards and even your yearbook. Make a list of all the clubs, teams, groups, and organizations you've joined over the years. Circle the ones that made you feel you belonged.

WHAT'S IN A NAME?

Consider the affectionate nicknames others have for you. List the ones you especially appreciate and the ways they may speak to your passions and character.

GOOD ENOUGH

Passion, check. Abilities, check. Perfection...hold on. Good and fulfilling may be good enough. Remind yourself that you're only human. Is there something you enjoy that you've been avoiding because your skills aren't at the level you feel they need to be? What can you do to sharpen your abilities in that area? Can you take a class, read a book, enlist a mentor? How can you explore the possibilities without letting feelings of inadequacy hold you back?

JUST ONE THING

Ask some of the closest, most-trusted people in your life: What is the one specific thing you appreciate most that I've done for you? It's a tough question that may require some thought, so be willing to wait for an answer—either in conversation or in written form, whatever is most comfortable for each of you.

No one is
useless in this world
who lightens the
burdens of another.

CHARLES DICKENS

In order to bring out the best in people, you need to give them your best.

OMAR SULEIMAN

BEHIND THE BONDS

How have you forged lasting connections in your life? Think about how you have met some of your closest friends and how those connections have grown. What would everyone say was the one thing about you that drew them to you? Are you the encourager in your circle? A good listener? A risk-taker who challenges others and stretches them? Are you a peacemaker who brings calm? What do you spark in your relationships with others?

WHAT YOU KNOW

This chapter's last question may be the simplest and the toughest at the same time. Listen to your inner voice for the answer, and trust what you know deep inside. What do you see or understand better than most people?

YOUR VALUES

How You See the World

Find guidance to claim a path with vision and personal meaning.

ON A MAGICAL MISSION

If you could wave a magic wand and change five things about your community, what would they be? Be specific—go much deeper than "Make it a better place to live." You could focus on aspects of education, schools, housing, or sustainability, to name a few. Where does your heart lead you?

POWERFUL ART

What media (books, songs, movies, artwork, and more) have really spoken to you? Describe how each made you feel and any actions you took as a result.

A MODEL FOR LIFE

While each of our lives, paths, and purposes are unique, we can look to others to strike a chord or ignite a spark. Whose life and accomplishments inspire you? It could be someone well known or someone in your inner circle.

What underlying traits or values draw you?

At times our own light goes out and is rekindled by a spark from another person.

ALBERT SCHWEITZER

YOUR LIVING LIST

List 20 things on your bucket list.

1.

2.

3.

4.

5.

6.

7.

8.

9.

10.

11.

12.

13.

14.

15.

16.

17.

18.

19.

20.

Now go back and circle the wishes with impact that would be felt beyond just your life.

EXAMINE YOUR SPENDING

You may already be investing in your values and piloting toward a purposeful path. What organizations or causes have you donated time or money to over the past few years?

NO GOING BACK

Whether big or small, what learning, experience, or revelation changed your life in some way?

WHAT'S TUGGING AT YOU?

A restless heart and mind may be trying to send a message. If you're having a difficult time falling asleep, what is keeping you up?

Every great dream begins with a dreamer.

HARRIET TUBMAN

THE PURPOSE IN THE WHY

Questions that haunt us can lead to directions to pursue. What unanswered questions in your life or in the larger world bother you?

GOOD GOSSIP

We love to say we don't care what others think. But reflecting on others' impressions of you can help you focus on what values and traits you hold in high esteem. Ask yourself: What do you want people to say about you when you're not around?

You have to be burning with an idea or a problem or a wrong that you want to right.

STEVE JOBS

WORTH FIGHTING FOR

We all have our line in the sand. What issues do you just have to stand up for when someone opposes your point of view?

ROOM FOR IMPROVEMENT

We don't bother putting time and energy into areas of our lives and selves that don't matter to us. So what traits have you been trying to improve in the past year?

What you focus on expands.

UNKNOWN

NO MATTER

Knowing what you don't value can be as powerful as knowing what you do. What part of your week always feels like a waste of time?

LET'S COMMENCE

Imagine you are the speaker at a commencement ceremony. What advice and inspiration do you offer? List your three top messages.

1.

2.

3.

OPEN YOUR TREASURE CHEST

Of all the things you own, what five items—or category of items—do you care about most? List them here. Below each item, write what it symbolizes to you.

1.

2.

3.

4.

5.

The world is so rich, simply throbbing with rich treasures, beautiful souls, and interesting people.

HENRY MILLER

I know nothing in the world that has as much power as a word.

EMILY DICKINSON

MORE THAN WORDS

Spiritual practices such as yoga and meditation often recommend reciting a mantra. It could be a single word or a short phrase that holds meaning for you and helps you focus. What words resonate with you? What would you choose as a mantra?

THE VALUES MENU

Whether we realize it or not, we prioritize certain values every time we make a decision. What 10 values rise to the top for you? Circle them. What three are the most essential along your path in life? Mark them with a star.

Acceptance	Courage	Happiness
Accountability	Creativity	Harmony
Action	Curiosity	Honesty
Adventure	Determination	Humor
Authenticity	Excellence	Imagination
Balance	Fairness	Independence
Beauty	Faith	Individuality
Challenge	Friendships	Integrity
Commitment	Frugality	Joy
Community	Fun	Justice
Compassion	Generosity	Kindness
Contribution	Grace	Knowledge
Conviction	Growth	Leadership

Learning
Logic
Love
Loyalty
Modesty
Openness
Optimism
Organization
Originality
Patience
Peace
Perseverance
Recognition
Reputation
Resilience
Respect
Responsibility
Security
Self-awareness
Self-reliance
Self-respect
Service
Simplicity
Sincerity
Spirituality
Stability
Strength
Success
Trustworthiness
Wealth
Wisdom

REINFORCE THE IMPORTANCE

For the top three values you identified on the Values Menu, make a plan to commit more fully to them in your everyday life. For example, if knowledge was one you picked, your Action Steps might include reading two books each month.

VALUE	ACTION STEPS
....	....
	....
	....
....	....
	....
	....
....	....
	....
	....

YOUR MESSAGE TO THE WORLD

If you had one 30-second commercial on TV, what message would it present?

WHAT'S YOUR MARK?

Imagine that you needed to introduce yourself and illustrate all that is important to you through a tattoo or a charm on a necklace. Draw what it would look like.

Be yourself; everyone else is already taken.

OSCAR WILDE

LOOK BACK

Write a journal entry dated five years from today. Where is the source of your joy and fulfillment? What is filling your hours?

YOUR POSSIBILITIES

Where You Can Make a Difference

Get inspiration for how you can dare to live fully for yourself and the world.

CALLING FOR YOU

This week, keep a record of all the times someone asks you for help—whether it's a small favor or a huge endeavor. As part of this exercise, jot down how you feel at the initial request and while following through. Are you excited, frustrated, challenged? Finally, capture the results. Were you able to provide the support needed?

REQUEST	FEELINGS	RESULTS

REQUEST	FEELINGS	RESULTS

OFF THE BACK BURNER

Is there something in your life you've always wanted to do but for some reason put on the back burner? It could be traveling to a certain destination, taking a class, or reaching out to a person who made an impact on your life. No more excuses! Make a step toward pursuing it this week—purchase the airline ticket, sign up for the class, write a letter. What's your next move?

SEE THE NEEDS

How many times do we see a situation and think, "I wish I could do something"? As you watch the news, scan your social feeds, and walk through your neighborhood this week, be alert. Where do you feel a pull to take action? You don't need to have the answers, just a realization of the need for answers or change.

YOU CAN'T LOSE

Fear of failure can stop us from ever starting a new endeavor. What would you do if you knew you couldn't fail?

Everything you want is on the other side of fear.

JACK CANFIELD

It is impossible to live
without failing at
something, unless you
live so cautiously
that you might as well
not have lived at all,
in which case you
have failed by default.

J. K. ROWLING

NO REGRETS

Think of a few times you held back from what your gut wanted you to do. How did it turn out? Does it still weigh on your mind?

OWN YOUR DREAM

You've probably seen those memes organized into quadrants that joke about what other people think we do with our time. But they bring up a good point: Parents, partners, and others in our lives do make assumptions about our passions and place expectations on us. Is there a dream you need to release because it was someone else's dream for you? Let go of it here.

TAKE BACK THE *NOT*

Many of us get a feeling at an early age that we want to be or do something in the world, only to be told it's *not* realistic, *not* the smart path, *not* a good job, *not* something that people actually do for a living. List all the *not* phrases you can recall being told, then cross out the *not* to open your life to the possibilities again.

PERFECT FITS

What is working well for you in your life—what do you find fulfilling, meaningful, enjoyable, and important?

CUT IT OUT

What isn't working well for you in your life and career—what drains you, makes you stressed and anxious, or wastes your time?

THE HIDDEN GIFT

Is there a skill or talent you have that you've never shared with anyone else? Detail a plan to step out and offer it to the world in some small way this week.

Many people die with their music still in them.

OLIVER WENDELL HOLMES

Nothing in life is to be feared, it is only to be understood.

MARIE CURIE

ESCAPE THE GRIP

Financial loss, compromised reputation, wasted time...all these risks and more can hold us back from pursuing our passions and callings. What fears hold you back? What steps can you take to begin to let go?

FEAR	FIRST STEPS

TRUE MEASURES

Try to outnumber your fears from page 114 with a list of all that you (and others!) have to gain when you're in touch with and following your purpose.

There is no greater gift you can give or receive than to honor your calling.

OPRAH WINFREY

It is the ultimate luxury to combine passion and contribution. It's also a very clear path to happiness.

SHERYL SANDBERG

HERE AND NOW

Think of a time when you felt truly significant and that all was right with the world in that moment. Where were you? What were you doing?

THE GREATNESS INSIDE

We may be striving for greatness when we've already found it. Has anyone ever told you that you're "great with... [fill in the blank]"? It could be animals, children, problem-solving, your hands. The list goes on. Write the words you've heard and take them to heart.

BRINGING IT ALL TOGETHER

Identify the sweet spot where your passions, gifts, and values meet the world's needs.

WHAT'S NEXT?

While there's no magic formula to calculate your ikigai, you can rest assured that you've done some of the hardest work in the preceding pages. You've looked back, looked forward, peeled away the layers, and revealed the real you. You've put in the time and dedication to realizing your purpose in this world.

Likely, patterns have emerged from your answers to the journal questions and prompts. In fact, it may help to go back over the pages and circle or highlight key words and ideas that seem to pop up again and again. Note what stands out for you when you consider:

- Your Passions
- Your Gifts
- Your Values
- Your Possibilities

Write your answers into the appropriate segments of the circle diagram on the next page. Try to narrow your selections in each area to three to five words or insights.

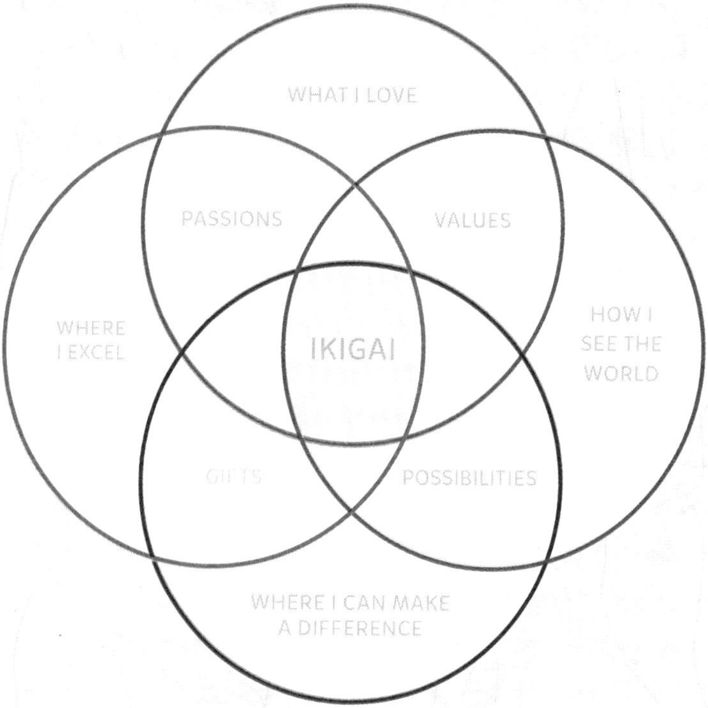

Ask yourself: Are there places of natural overlap—where your answers can fit under one umbrella or lead down one common path? *That's your ikigai!* And it's quite different—yet equally powerful—for everyone.

One person may find clusters that identify strengths in teaching and repairing, a passion for children and education, values of sustainability and equal access to opportunities, and a need for eco-friendly, affordable transportation in the world. Her ikigai may look like teaching families to refurbish and repair bikes at a shop or community center.

Another person may have a passion for yoga, the experience of bouncing back from job losses, and a concern for those struggling with anxiety. His ikigai may suggest coaching job candidates to ace interviews by preparing with breathing techniques.

Knowing your ikigai is just the start. What will you do with that opportunity—can it supply a living, or will it simply be enough to provide purpose for you each day? Coming to that answer may take some time and reflection. But before you lose the momentum, what is one thing you can do to honor your ikigai...

Today? ______________________________

____

This week? ______________________________

____

This month? ______________________________

____

This year? ______________________________

____